Barry Campbell

Barry Campbell

Performers in Uniform

THE SILVER EAGLES

By Peter B. Mohn

Photographs courtesy of the
U.S. Army

 CHILDRENS PRESS, CHICAGO

Library of Congress Cataloging in Publication Data

Mohn, Peter B.
  The Silver Eagles.

  (Performers in uniform)
  Includes index.
  SUMMARY: Discusses the activities of the Army
helicopter demonstration team known as the Silver Eagles.
  [1. United States. Army Aviation Precision
Demonstration Team. 2. Stunt flying. 3. Helicopters.
4. Aeronautics, Military]1. United States. Army
Aviation Precision Demonstration Team—Juvenile
literature. 2. Stunt flying—Juvenile literature.
2. Military helicopters—Juvenile literature.
I. Title.
UG1233.M63   797.5′4   77-27728
ISBN 0-516-01953-8

THE MAN WHO TALKS TO HELICOPTERS

The Army Silver Eagles were doing their show. But what was *that* helicopter doing there?

It was blue and white, like the others. But this was no ordinary helicopter. It wore a hat on its plexiglass bubble. It had eyes that rolled, a red mouth, and floppy ears. A red light winked from one of its skids, and a siren whined.

Captain Ron Cox, the Silver Eagles announcer, asked, "Hey, what are you doing there?"

In answer, the chopper hooked its skids into a banner on the ground and lifted it. "Bozo," the banner read.

"Oh, so you're Bozo," Cox said. "Well, Bozo, we have a show to do here. You are holding things up. Take your banner and get out of here."

Bozo dipped and flew off in a cloud of smoke.

"Now, we'd like to show you one of the acts we developed ourselves," said Captain Cox to the crowd. Six blue and white helicopters appeared out of nowhere.

"Please watch as the Silver Eagles perform their unique 'Keystone Cop Scramble'," said Captain Cox.   Looking like they could collide at any moment, the choppers twisted and spun. They flew so close together some people in the crowd found themselves covering their eyes. The moves completed, they flew off to regroup for the next part of the air show.

Soon two more helicopters sped into show center. As Captain Cox described their flight, they spiraled upward, coming ever closer together. Then they separated, turned, and flew directly toward each other. From the ground it seemed as though they passed each other with only inches to spare.

"Now, the Silver Eagles . . . Bozo, are you back again?"
Captain Cox said as the audience laughed. The clown
helicopter had a large round object attached to its skid.
"What have you there, Bozo?"

The striped round thing began to fall.

"Oh, I see," said Captain Cox, "You have a yo-yo."

Indeed Bozo did. The only difference between his yo-yo
and the yo-yos people use was that his was one meter (3.28
feet) in diameter. It weighed almost 220 kilograms (485
pounds). It dropped to the end of its "string" and began to
rise again. Bozo flew straight up, hoping to help the giant
yo-yo. Suddenly however, the yo-yo spun. It lost its
momentum and stopped.

"Okay, Bozo, nice try. Now get out of here." said Captain
Cox. Bozo turned on his smoke and flew off. All during the
Silver Eagles show, Bozo would return to bedevil Captain
Cox. He acted as though he wanted to delay the Eagles'
show. He was really part of it.

"Bozo is the only clown helicopter in the country," Cox
told the crowd. "You may notice that he only comes in when
there's a little break in the rest of the show.

"Chief Warrant Officer Richard 'Hob' Hobson flies Bozo.
And seated next to him as his copilot is a bright orange
teddy bear."

The clown helicopter returned again and again. Each time,
Cox pretended to be more angry with him. Then, suddenly, it
looked like Bozo was in trouble.

7

Five helicopters had him surrounded. Bozo turned completely around. There was a Silver Eagle on every side.

"They've got you now," Cox chuckled. If a helicopter could look worried, Bozo did. He began a slow climb. The other five climbed with him. His siren became quiet. The helicopters climbed to 50, then 100, then 200 feet above the ground. The crowd waited. What would happen now?

"That's all for you, Bozo," Cox said. "We have you where we want you."

All at once, a big puff of white smoke came from Bozo's tailpipe. The siren started to wail again. And Bozo dove toward the earth, flying out from under his "jail."

Cox turned to the crowd. "Well, he's done it again," he said. The crowd laughed and applauded. "What do you do to a clown when you catch him anyway?"

In the last part of the Silver Eagle show, Bozo flew to the top of a pyramid formed by the others. When the group landed, his pilot joined the other six on the flight line.

"Bozo never starts the show with the rest," Cox said. "We park the Bozo helicopter way down the flight line. The first time he appears, it should be a surprise for the crowd."

"The helicopter is no different from the others," Hobson explained. "We add the eyes, ears, nose, mouth, and siren just for the shows. When we're flying from site to site, that stuff comes off."

Hobson was only the third person to fly Bozo. In 1976, Chief Warrant Officer Bill Hillard became the fourth.

"Bozo looks almost human in what he does," Hillard said. "Part of this is because I know what the narrator is saying to me. It really makes it look good when I can rock or dip the chopper and answer yes or no a few times.

"But no matter how it looks, Bozo is flying. It's the same kind of flying I'd do in combat, or in peacetime. I'm too busy flying to watch the crowd, and the chopper makes too much noise for me to hear anything."

HELICOPTERS IN PEACE AND WAR

"The helicopter is just a baby in military terms," a Silver Eagle said. "But oh, what a baby!"

The first fixed-wing aircraft were flown in 1914 during World War I. They were very simple machines. By World War II, bigger, more complicated aircraft had been added. Until then, the Air Force was part of the Army.

Then the Army Air Corps, as it had been known, was separated from the Army. The new Air Force took the heavy bombers and jet fighters. Army Aviation kept troop transports and light observation aircraft.

"No aircraft has had so many uses as the helicopter," said Lieutenant Colonel Ben Powell, Silver Eagle "boss."

"It's an ideal bird for rescues. We use them that way in the Army. So do the Coast Guard, the Navy, the Air Force, and hundreds of fire and police departments.

"It's good for lifting things," Powell continued. "We haul things light and heavy with the CH-54 'Flying Crane.' Civilian builders use them for lifting things into out-of-the-way places on tall buildings."

"Let me tell you. A helicopter can be anything you want it to—almost," Captain Cox added.

"Police use them for searches and traffic control. Hospitals use them for ambulances, like we do in wartime. With the right equipment, they fight forest fires. They are used in taking aerial photographs.

"Any aircraft that can land and take off in a small space, climb straight up, land straight down, and hover has to be useful," Cox added.

"Some of the first helos the Army flew are very famous," Rowell said. "The television show 'M*A*S*H' features some of the first choppers the Army had. They had gasoline engines, and three men could sit in the cockpit.

"There wasn't room for a wounded man inside, so they built shelters above the skids for them. Helicopters carried a lot of wounded men in the Korean conflict."

"By the 1960s we had many more kinds of choppers," Hillard said. "We had the Huey, the Kiowa, and the much bigger Chinook to transport troops. The Cobra was loaded with guns and could lay in a lot of fire on the enemy."

The Silver Eagles fly a helicopter called the OH6, or "Cayuse." It's one of the smallest choppers the Army has.

"It's also one of the fastest," Cox said. "The OH6 has held speed, altitude, and distance records. For us, it's best because it's very economical. Its engine is really very small.

"The OH6 is a light observation helicopter," Cox said. "In combat, they might be used to find the enemy. Then other, more heavily armed aircraft can be called in to attack. Sometimes, the observers in the OH6 would be used to direct artillery fire."

Powell noted that all the Silver Eagle pilots had served in Vietnam.

AH-IG Cobra

CH-47A Chinook

OH-58 Kiowa

The OH6 helicopters the Silver Eagles fly are also combat veterans. "Before we got these machines, they were junk or close to it. They had been wrecked in one way or another. We brought them home and rebuilt them.

"You can look at any one of the helicopters and find places where bullet holes have been patched. Maybe thousands of man-hours have gone into them. They've been given lots of work, and they show it.

"We don't believe in machines that don't work. In fact, our whole performance is designed to show how many things this machine can do."

OOHS, AAHS, AND BILLOWING SMOKE

The Silver Eagles air show is a combination of things. Some of the parts show how exactly a helicopter can be flown. Others show the beauty of flight. Bozo provides the laughs. And some maneuvers appear scary to the crowds.

"They don't scare us," a pilot said. "We're up there. We know what we're doing."

Much of the time, the helicopters trail white smoke. It's made by dripping a special oil into the exhaust of their jet engines. The heat turns the oil to smoke.

"A lot of people are worried by the smoke," Cox said. "We use Corvus oil to make it. This oil has been around for years. It's used in crop spraying and many other ways. It's non-polluting and bio-degradable. It might not smell the best, but it isn't hurting anything."

The Silver Eagles solo pilots draw their share of oohs and aahs.

"In many solo maneuvers, the two aircraft fly right at each
other. They start at opposite ends of the field and meet at
the center," Chief Warrant Officer Hillard explained. "They
have the best chance to show what these helicopters can
do."

"Most people think of helicopters flying straight and
level," Cox added. "They do most of the time. A light, fast
aircraft like the OH6 we fly can do more, however. We
show what it can be made to do."

The Silver Eagle show begins like others with the "walkdown." The six pilots walk down the flight line in step. When each gets to his aircraft, he breaks off. He exchanges salutes with his crew chief. Together they make a quick check of the craft from the outside.

Then the pilot climbs in. The crew chief helps the pilot put on his helmet and shoulder harness. On a radio signal from Powell, the leader, they "crank" or start their engines.

"Only six of the aircraft are on the flight line," Hobson, the Bozo pilot, said. "I'm down with the spare chopper. We're listening on the radio. When the Boss says crank, we crank too."

"Every once in a while, one of our machines on the flight line won't crank. Or the pilot will see that something is wrong. If that happens, the pilot jumps out, runs to a car and goes down to the spare," Cox explained.

"The ailing helicopter is shut down. The pilot in the spare takes off at the same time as the others and joins the formation before the first maneuver," he added.

Soon after takeoff, all six helicopters fly directly toward the crowd.

"Our first and last maneuvers are perhaps the most spectacular," Cox said. "The first is the Starburst. The pilots turn their smoke on at a signal from the leader. On the count, each one breaks out of formation in a different direction.

"The smoke trails leave a six-pointed star in the sky, if it isn't blown around too badly by the wind. After the Starburst, the solos do their Hammerheads. Then it's Bozo's turn."

The demonstration of the six choppers has a little of everything.

"We even get a commercial in," Powell said. "We start by taking a page out of Bozo's book. Each chopper picks up a banner. We all lift off together so the letters on the banners seem to spell "ARMGOY" at first.

"Two of us climb higher. When it's right, it reads, 'Go Army.'

"We have another set that reads 'Go Navy.' We aren't just entertainers or performers. We try to help recruiters get young men and women to join the service."

The Silver Eagles show is not a show of stunts, Powell said. "We don't do things with our aircraft that other helicopter pilots can't. We show precision flying and no more."

It is estimated that the width of one rotor blade separates the blades of the aircraft in formation. "We fly forward and backward and close together," Powell said. "Some of our maneuvers might remind the crowd of people square dancing. Others? I don't know."

One of the square dancing maneuvers might be the "pylon pivot," as the Eagles call it. Two lines of three aircraft each face one another. They fly closer, holding their lines. They pass, and when they've passed, each makes a left turn at the same time. Each line flies back to its starting point.

"After that, the helicopters set down," Cox said. "They then take off backwards. That's to show one of the things a helicopter can do."

One of the hardest maneuvers for spectators to watch is the "Keystone Cop Scramble."

"In this, each pilot flies a pattern. We circle in and around one another. We don't use much space to do it, so it looks like we're trying to wrap one aircraft around the next," said Captain Gary Pinnette of the 1976 team.

"I don't know how many times I've said it," added Chief Warrant Officer Bill Darnell, 1975 wingman. "Once we have the routine down, it isn't stunt flying. It's just plain flying."

"There are other parts that are hard to explain," Cox added. "What's happening in the air is different from what the crowd thinks it's seeing.

"Some of the things the solos do are a good example. The crowd stands at least 1,500 feet back from the flight line. That creates an optical illusion. Most people can't tell from that distance if there's 20 feet between the solos or 100.

"I'll tell you one thing," he said. "They're close enough. Going almost 150 miles per hour, the solo aircraft come from opposite sides to show center. Almost like some jet teams, they rotate their aircraft almost 90 degrees as they pass," Cox said. "We rotate to show both the speed and the maneuverability of the helicopter."

"And on others, we do things because we think they're just plain pretty. The Starburst is one. Another one is the Umbrella. We climb in formation, then each one goes in a different direction. It looks like the spokes of an umbrella."

There are three different shows in the Eagles' book.

"We have what we call our high show, a low show, and a point show," Lieutenant Colonel Powell explained. "The high show is the full one. It has all the parts in it. If the weather isn't too good, we can go to a low show. We take some of the vertical things out. And a point show is done when we don't have enough space to do all our maneuvers."

When the show, whatever the kind, is over, the helicopters return to the flight line. Bozo joins them as they land. When the engines are shut down, the pilots get out and walk back up the flight line.

Captain Ron Cox names the pilots and ground crews for each of the helicopters as they get out. "I'm proud of that," he said. "I decided when I started as narrator that it would look better if I could name them all from memory. So I did. And I do, and I get their home towns right, too."

The show is over, but the Silver Eagles aren't done.

PENMEN, NOT SWORDSMEN

More than 100 people stood around the pilots. Some just wanted their signatures. Many told them how much they'd enjoyed the show. Others asked questions about the team, the helicopters, and the Army.

No one who wants it goes away from a Silver Eagles autograph session without a complete set of signatures.

"We come to fly, of course," Powell said. "But we also come to meet as many people as we can. Signing autographs is one way of doing that."

Specialist Fourth Class Paul Holman stood near the pilots. He had a sheaf of photographs in his hands. He passed them out to anyone who wanted one.

"You can start with Captain Cox. He's right over there," he told one youngster. The boy presented the picture to Cox, who signed his name.

"I want to learn to fly just like you do," said a very young boy at Cox's feet. He handed his picture to Cox, who signed it. Then Cox squatted down and grinned at the youngster.

"Well, thank you very much," he said. "I hope you do. I hope you join the Army when you grow up."

"I will," the boy said. "My Dad's in the Army now."

"At a show with a lot of people, we may be autographing long after the show is over," Cox said.

The crowd around the pilots finally left.

"Five minutes," Powell told another pilot. "Pass the word." In five minutes, the pilots left the show area. They climbed into cars and drove back to their motel. In one of their rooms, they watched a videotape of their show and talked about it.

"We had a good one today," Powell said. "The wind was right, the sky was clear, and the crowd was good. Anybody have anything to say?" No one did. Cox handed Powell some papers.

"It says here we go picnicking with the Scouts tonight," Powell said. "Casual clothes, I guess, and we should be there by six. Anyone know where this place is?" No one did.

"How does it happen that we can find our way all over the United States and into Canada, and no one knows his way around a medium-sized town in Indiana?" Powell laughed.

"We're driving, not flying," said one of the pilots. "Without flight control, we're lost." The pilots returned to their rooms for some relaxation before their evening began.

"For every show we fly, we probably have two breakfasts, one lunch, and some kind of formal dinner to go to," Powell said. "It's hectic but it's fun.

"We could fly all over the country and see the sights. That would be one thing. But we meet an awful lot of people and that makes it much more interesting and much more fun."

At the picnic, each member of the team was assigned a host. Many home-made dishes—baked beans, salads and casseroles—sat on tables for all to share, but it was each host's duty to cook hot dogs for his Eagle over his own fire.

"This is great!" exclaimed a Silver Eagle ground crewman. "Some places we go, all they can think of is banquets with steaks, roast beef, or chicken. Back at Fort Rucker (home of the Silver Eagles in Alabama), we get Army cooking. I love this home cooking."

Throughout the picnic, pilots and ground crewmen sat, ate, and talked.

"It gives me a good feeling at times like these," a pilot said. "I love to fly and I live to fly. But I love to be with people, too. "

Before the next show the following day, there were more visits. Groups of pilots and ground crewmen fanned out and saw people in hospitals, nursing homes and schools.

"We see everyone," a Silver Eagle said. "Sometimes the recruiters prefer only the young groups. Older people, though, have paid taxes for years. They're our bosses."

If the recruiters have young people interested in joining the Army, there may be a special meeting.

"We try to help them make up their minds," Powell said. "We know that not everyone who joins the Army will go for flying. Most of us, however, didn't start out in the aviation program. We try to show them that we think the Army's a good place to be."

THE MAKING OF AN EAGLE

"I haven't always been a helicopter pilot," Captain Cox said. "I wasn't always an officer, either.

"I enlisted in the Army and went through basic training like almost everyone else. I became a specialist—I worked for the doctors in clinics."

Cox said he had the chance to become an officer and took it. After Officer Candidate School, he went into the Army flight program. After more than a year of training, he graduated. That was 1967.

"After that, almost every Army pilot could expect some Vietnam duty," he continued. "I got mine." He flew helicopter gunships over Vietnam for 26 months. In his years of flying, he qualified to fly six different Army choppers.

Late in 1973, the Army called for volunteers for the Silver Eagles.

Captain Cox

"That interested me," Cox noted. "It meant that we'd be out meeting people and showing our interest in the Army. I thought I'd enjoy that so I volunteered and made it!"

"One of the nice parts of this group is that it isn't exactly an officer's club," a ground crewman said. "The Army has drawn many pilots from among enlisted men. When a man graduates from the flight program, he becomes an officer. It's another way of getting ahead."

The Eagles' nest is at Fort Rucker, Alabama. Every year, a number of pilots volunteer for the Silver Eagles. From them, a much smaller group is chosen.

"We get the men around us late in the season," Powell said. "They get a chance to look us over, and we look them over—very carefully."

"If a man isn't qualified to fly the OH6, he qualifies. He may even do some flying with the team, but he won't fly shows. Toward the end of the show season, we select the new team members."

Cox pointed out that the men also have to be chosen for their part on the team. "We try to put a pilot where he'll do the best job," he said. "The way a diamond pilot flies is different from a solo job, or from Bozo. The leader has to make good and careful decisions. We know we're getting the best pilots. Choosing the best pilot for a certain job is another matter."

Silver Eagles have seldom gone from one year to the next with the same show. Each year during the training period, new parts of the show may be introduced.

"Sometimes you'd think you were putting a new football play together," a pilot said. "Someone will come up with an idea for a new maneuver. We'll talk about it first. He'll diagram it on the blackboard. Then, if it still looks good, we'll go out and fly it.

"There were no helicopter teams when the Eagles were organized. They couldn't do all the same things the jet groups do. So our men played it by ear."

"The first group of Silver Eagles got together for one show only," Powell chuckled. "When they were done with the show, everyone thought they would disband. They didn't. So those of us who followed them have had to put new and more exciting things into our show.

"Most of the ideas come from the pilots themselves. They're not all good, either. We have done something all season, then watched the videotapes and said that it just didn't work. So we've thrown it out and put in something else."

Between the first of the year and the start of the show season, the Silver Eagles practice.

"It's kind of like learning how to follow the leader," a wingman said. "The leader is the Boss. He flies his helicopter and the rest of us keep up with him."

Once or twice a day, the pilots go through the routine. After, they debrief and talk about the show. More comments are made by the narrator and other people who stayed on the ground.

"We work a lot on the close stuff," a pilot said. "We start out with the aircraft rather far apart. As we get more used to the routine and each other, we get closer together."

The pilots work on timing for their opposing maneuvers, also staying farther apart at first.

"And Bozo goes off by himself and plays with his barrel, his hoops, and his yo-yo," Hillard laughed. "That yo-yo is a bearcat. I have enough trouble with the small kind you spin from your hand."

After the maneuvers are perfected, the Eagles have more to do. "We know we can't take more than a certain amount of time in every show," Powell explained. "Before we go on the road, we must get our timing right. We have to put the show together and make sure that the solos do their work at the right time, and that Bozo doesn't take too much.

"When we can take just about a half hour from walkdown to landing, we've got it just about right," he added.

There's more than the routine to be done in the off-season. New green and silver flight suits must be tailored for the Eagles. Hundreds of photos are taken and publicity is set up.

"The ground crews have as much to learn as the pilots," a crew chief said. "If one of the aircraft can't fly, we have to fix it. Quickly. They all have to be kept shining."

Finally, in late March, the Silver Eagles get ready. The "Boss" gives his men a little time off, because the season is long and they'll be away from Fort Rucker for long periods of time. The first show of the year usually goes on during the first weekend of April.

ON THE ROAD IN THE SKY

"We aren't the best-known team in the air shows, but we're the slowest," said a Silver Eagle, laughing.

The tiny OH6 helicopter may be one of the Army's faster helicopters, but it wasn't made for long,cross-country flights. It can't carry much fuel. And it's uncomfortable to fly for long periods.

"The Blue Angels or the Thunderbirds may go a thousand miles in a few hours," Powell said. "It will take us a few days."

"I don't mind," said another pilot. "We get to see the sights, and this is a beautiful country."

Two people—the pilot and the crew chief—travel in each of the aircraft. The rest of the crew travels in their transport plane, a Caribou, except for two men. They drive a black and silver van from show site to show site. The van carries some of the Eagles' ground markers, some of Bozo's "toys," and the public address system.

"Some of our trips may keep us out three weeks at a time," Powell said. "We don't get to see our families as much. We don't have the time, and can't afford the fuel, to go home between dates.

"The Caribou has helped that. After a certain time, we may park the helicopters at a show site, climb into the plane and go back to Fort Rucker for a couple of days. The Caribou isn't a fast airplane. But it'll carry us all and it's fast enough."

Flying from site to site in the OH6 isn't all that bad, according to one crew chief. "In my first year as crew chief, my pilot and I were going from Fort Rucker to the first show site. He asked if I knew how to fly the helicopter. I thought I could, and told him so.

" 'Well, take it, then,' he said. I put my hands on the controls and my feet on the pedals. He began coaching me a little. Pretty soon, I was flying the aircraft.

"Now when we go from site to site, I almost always do the flying. The pilot's always there if something goes wrong, but I have learned a lot in the past year or two."

At first, the crew chief said, he wasn't sure if his pilot was doing him a special favor in letting him fly. "It turned out that all the other crew chiefs were flying too," he added. "Now, if we have to move an aircraft from one spot to another, the crew chiefs just do it. We won't bother the pilots with the short hop stuff."

"My crew chief can fly from site to site. He can probably take care of the aircraft much better than I. But I'm still the only one who's going to fly it in the shows," a Silver Eagle said.

If there's more than 300 or 400 miles between show sites, the Eagles may take two days or more to make the trip. Stopovers sometimes are made at military bases, and sometimes at commercial airfields.

"I guess we've surprised a few people by dropping in," Powell said. "It isn't every day that a horde of helicopters drops out of the sky to spend the night. This is another part of the fun of our job."

Sometimes, stops aren't planned.

"Every once in a while, something will go wrong with a helicopter in flight," Cox explained. "Once when we were traveling, one of them had an engine problem. We sat down right out in the middle of nowhere. We had the Hueys for support then, so they were right with us. Our crews changed the engine in the aircraft. It took them about an hour. We didn't miss our schedule by much, even with the engine change," Cox added.

Once at the new show site, schedules and housing assignments are handed out. Supplies and clothing are unloaded from the Caribou. Part of thc ground crew begins laying out the show site. Markers for the show are heavy metal plates painted several different colors.

"Doing the layout is sometimes easy and sometimes hard," a crewman said. "Sometimes they expect to have the show over tall grass. We have a lot of cutting to do before the markers can be seen. Most of the time, though, it's easy."

The markers are laid out accurately. Distances between each are measured. While some crewmen finish this job, others shine, refuel, and service the helicopters. Two men trundle a heavy barrel of Corvus oil around to fill the smoke oil tanks. One of the pilots marks an aerial photo of the show site to show the others where they'll be flying. Another pilot calls the Federal Aviation Administration to get the latest weather reports.

"We have our commitments to consider then," Cox said. "We schedule our people for banquets, picnics and visits. If there are other acts in the air show, we usually meet with them. Then, one or two days before the show, we give the press rides."

"We give rides to people who work for the newspapers, radio, and television," Cox explained. "Almost always, they write stories about us. We get people out to our shows from this kind of thing."

The riders are helmeted and stuffed into flight suits, and the doors are taken off the helicopters. Crewmen strap them into their seats. Earphones and microphones built into the helmets enable the riders to talk to their pilot.

"We try to give these people the chance to see what a typical flight is like," Cox said. "If the land around the airport is right, we might be able to show a little of how we fly in combat."

The press people are shown steep climbs and dives. The helicopters are made to hover, then they're flown at top speed. In some communities, almost all of the aircraft have been used, and radio broadcasts have been made from them.

"We'll do anything we can to help draw a crowd to our show," Powell said. "Almost everywhere we go, we'll fly over an area in our wedge formation, making smoke. It makes people wonder what's happening. That, plus publicity, makes bigger crowds."

LIFE IN A BUBBLE

Helicopters are noisy and they seem to vibrate a lot. And they must be flown all the time.

"It takes both hands and both feet to fly a helicopter," Cox said. "The pilot's right hand controls rotor attitude. He can pull or push the control in any direction. If he pushes the right hand forward, the aircraft goes forward. If he pulls back, it goes backward."

The left hand of the pilot controls the pitch of the rotor. The pitch control is by the side of the seat he sits on. If there's no pitch on the rotor, the helicopter won't fly. When the pilot lifts the control and pitch is applied, the helicopter will rise.

And the feet go on pedals that control the small tail rotor, which is used to turn the aircraft.

There's almost no chatter on the radio during a Silver Eagles show. Usually, only the team leader and the lead solo pilot talk at all from the aircraft. The only other voice on the radio is that of one of the ground crewmen.

To listen, it sounds more like they'd gone out for a Sunday drive. "Right turn . . . now. Left turn . . . now. Smoke on . . . now," said the team leader as the team went through a maneuver. He spoke quietly. There was no excitement in his voice.

"We go through this so many times, there's no reason to be excited," Powell explained.

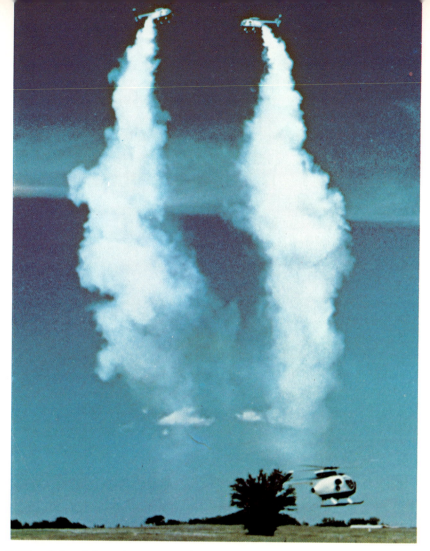

"The big thing is to concentrate. You have to be particular about where you are. Some times, you keep up with the Boss. Other times, you watch for a marker on the ground," a wingman added. When the solo pilots are performing, the radio is still rather quiet.

"Flying solo is more a matter of timing," explained a pilot. "The two pilots want to be sure they meet at show center. This means they must be at the outer marks at the same time and going the same speed."

Perhaps the most talkative of all on the radio is the ground crewman.

"The Bozo pilot must respond to the narrator," said Sergeant First Class Doug DeVoe. "When the narrator says something, I repeat it on the radio, and Bozo does his thing. He has to do it quickly or it isn't as funny, so I relay everything almost as it's being said."

"When we're regrouping the Diamond, we can't see what's going on at show center," Powell continued. "If Bozo is in there, we can tell by what the ground crewman is saying how soon we can go back on."

"I think they could just about do a show without the radio," Cox said. "The one thing radio does is make things a lot tighter. Our timing is much better than it would be without radio."

"It also helps in tight formations," another pilot said. "The Boss flies out front. He can't see everything all the time. If the formation gets out of whack, the man in the slot can see it all and say so."

All the Silver Eagle pilots agreed that flying a show wearies them.

"When I land, I feel a little tired," one said. "I'm not tired like I might be after running the mile. But a mile runner wouldn't get tired like I do, either. I really can't get ready to fly another show until the next day, though."

ASK THE "BOSS"

"If you take a group like this, you'll always find a bunch of nice guys," a Silver Eagle crewman said. "But the whole thing—whether they're good or bad—rests on the shoulders of the Boss."

"I have a fun job," Powell said, "But sometimes I have to stop and remember it's a big one."

The Silver Eagles team numbers about 40. Powell not only leads the helicopters in flight, he commands the whole team.

"You have to like a job like this," he said. "Otherwise, it would drive you nuts."

The Silver Eagles leader begins his year by attending the scheduling conference. At this conference, involving all the performers in uniform, show dates are set.

"There are hundreds of air shows every year. Some are big and some are small. They ask each year for appearances by us, the Blue Angels, the Thunderbirds, and the Golden Knights. Every year, the leaders all get together and decide who goes where," Powell explained.

He added that he thought the two Army teams were a bit luckier than some of the others. "Take the Blues or the Thunderbirds. They have to have long runways at their show sites or nearby. Their shows are speed shows. They take a lot of space.

"The Eagles can just about do their thing on a football field. The Golden Knights (Army Parachute Team) can jump into even smaller spaces. The Army can go places the Navy and Air Force can't even dream of."

After the next year's schedule is set, the leader goes back to Fort Rucker.

"The next job is to begin training new pilots to the team. Often a holdover member will move from one job to another. This means we have some old members learning new jobs."

With the help of his executive officer, the leader also must handle the team's business.

"I have a lot of help, but when something has to be decided that's my job," Powell said. "I may not always make the decision, but I might have to back it up."

The year 1977 is Powell's twentieth in the Army. He became a pilot in 1959, and he flies both fixed-wing and rotor aircraft.

"The Army has been good to me," he said. "I've had a lot of good duty. I've been able to get more education, and I've enjoyed my turn with the Silver Eagles. I hope more Army pilots will have the chance to fly with the Eagles."

In 1976, it was clear that Powell would not see his wish come true. Early in the year, the Army decided to disband the Silver Eagles. They were costing too much. The team was ordered to break up after the show season was over.

"I guess we should have expected that," Powell said. "Face it. When the group was organized, it was for one show only. Then it got a year, then two. We've been taking it from one year to the next for a long time."

News of the Army's order spread.

"We must have made a lot of friends," Powell said. "We started getting letters saying the people wanted us. Some wrote to their congressmen and the President. I don't think anything that's happened in the past two years has meant so much to us.

"We still don't know if the team will ever perform again. I hope it does. Still, I think we've helped recruit good people for the Army and we've shown what Army professionals can do."

About the Author:

Peter B. Mohn published his first children's book in 1975. He still hasn't gotten over it. The **Silver Eagles** is his 5th book. A native of Minneapolis, he now lives in a small town in Minnesota. He is a lover of sailing and outdoor sports.

INDEX